Preface 3
Chapter 1: The Psychology of Trading: An Introduction 5
Chapter 2: The Emotional Rollercoaster: Understanding Your Trading Mindset 9
Chapter 3: Mastering Your Emotions: Controlling Fear and Greed 13
Chapter 4: Mastering Awareness and Emotional Balance 19
Chapter 5: Cognitive Biases and Trading: Overcoming Mental Pitfalls 25
Chapter 6: Developing a Disciplined Approach: The Importance of Self-Control 30
Chapter 7: The Role of Risk Perception: Balancing Caution and Opportunity 34
Chapter 8: Decision Making Under Pressure 38
Chapter 9: Building a Winning Mindset: Confidence and Resilience in Trading 42
Chapter 10: Managing Losses: Strategies for Dealing with Setbacks 46
Chapter 11: Trading and Self-Identity: Exploring the Personal Impact of Success and Failure 48
Chapter 12: The Social Aspect of Trading: Emotional Contagion and Herding Behavior 51
Chapter 13: Trading and Cognitive Performance: Enhancing Mental Sharpness 54
Chapter 14: Overcoming Analysis Paralysis: Finding Clarity in Information Overload 58
Chapter 15: The Role of Intuition in Trading: Trusting

Your Gut Instincts — 62
Chapter 16: Time Perspective and Trading: Balancing Short-Term and Long-Term Thinking — 66
Chapter 17: Trading Psychology and System Development: Aligning Strategies with Personal Traits — 69
Chapter18: Risk Management: Safeguarding Your Trading Journey — 73
Chapter 19: From Novice to Expert: The Psychology of Skill Acquisition in Trading — 76
Chapter 20: Beyond Profit and Loss: Finding Meaning and Fulfillment in Trading — 80
About the Author — 83

Trading from within: Unleashing your psychological edge

Preface

Welcome to the captivating world of financial markets, where trading can be both a thrilling adventure and a formidable challenge. As we embark on this journey together, it is crucial to understand that success in trading extends far beyond technical analysis and market knowledge. It requires a profound comprehension of the human mind and the psychological factors that influence decision-making.

Within the pages of "Trading from within: Unleashing your Psychological Edge," you will discover a comprehensive guide that explores the intricate relationship between psychology and trading. This book has been meticulously crafted to equip traders of all levels, whether seasoned or novice, with the essential tools needed to navigate the treacherous waters of the financial markets in a simple and engaging way.

By unraveling the complex psychological aspects that underpin trading, we will embark on a profound exploration of our own minds. We will develop strategies to enhance our performance by gaining valuable insights and practical techniques. Real-world examples will serve as guiding lights, illuminating the path to success.

Trading from within: Unleashing your psychological edge

Through this book, you will become the master of your mind, unleashing its potential for greatness in your trading journey. You will delve deep within yourself, confronting the stark reality of the world of probability. By embracing this truth, you will finally begin to unlock your psychological edge.

With the knowledge gained from these pages, you will be equipped to navigate the ever-changing landscape of the financial markets. You will not only achieve your trading goals but also maintain emotional well-being and fulfillment along the way.

Prepare yourself to embark on a transformative experience, as you search from within and harness the power of our own mind. Embrace the world of probability, for it holds the key to your success. Together, we will explore the depths of psychology and trading, empowering you to achieve greatness in the realm of financial markets.

Welcome to "Trading from within: Unleashing your Psychological Edge."

Chapter 1: The Psychology of Trading: An Introduction

Welcome to the captivating world of trading, where financial markets hold the promise of independence, excitement, and the opportunity to participate in the global economy. As you embark on this journey, it is crucial to recognize the significant influence of psychological factors on trading decisions. This chapter serves as the foundation for your exploration of these factors, inviting you to embark on a journey of self-discovery and self-improvement.

When individuals first enter the world of trading, they are often captivated by the allure of the "Rich Life" portrayed on social media platforms like Instagram, YouTube, and TikTok. However, they soon discover that trading is not easy money—it requires mastering not only the technical aspects but also the psychological aspects. It's not just about patterns and candlesticks; it's about how you react to the market. In fact, the psychological part of trading accounts for approximately 90% of mastering this craft.

In this book, we delve into the psychological factors that impact trading decisions. We explore the mindset required for success, and we invite you to join us on a journey of self-discovery and self-improvement. By understanding the inner workings of your mind and learning to navigate the psychological challenges of trading, you can unlock your full potential as a trader.

One of the key aspects we address is the importance of psychology in trading. While many may believe that trading is solely driven by cold, rational analysis, the truth is that emotions and cognitive biases play a significant role in shaping our trading behavior. Emotions such as fear, greed, overconfidence, and impulsiveness can lead to irrational decisions and detrimental outcomes. Understanding these psychological aspects is crucial for achieving long-term success in the markets.

In this book, we lay the foundation for your trading journey by delving into the psychological factors that impact trading decisions. We explore the mindset required for success, and we invite you to embark on a journey of self-discovery and self-improvement. By understanding the inner workings of your mind and learning to navigate the psychological challenges of trading, you can unlock your full potential as a trader.

We begin by discussing the mindset of a successful trader, focusing on the importance of discipline, self-control, and emotional resilience. Discipline is the bedrock of successful trading, allowing you to make rational decisions even in the face of uncertainty and market volatility. We provide practical strategies for overcoming impulsive behavior and the fear of missing out (FOMO).

The patient mindset

Patience is a virtue that every trader must embrace, as it helps withstand market fluctuations and resist the temptation of chasing quick profits. We discuss how patience contributes to staying focused on long-term goals and avoiding the pitfalls of impatience and instant gratification.

Instant Gratification

Instant gratification can have negative effects on the brain in the context of trading. When we seek immediate rewards and constantly chase the feeling of instant gratification, our brain's reward system becomes activated, releasing dopamine—a neurotransmitter associated with pleasure and motivation. This dopamine surge reinforces neural pathways related to seeking instant rewards, which can lead to addictive behavior patterns.

Over time, this addiction to instant gratification can impair our ability to make sound trading decisions. It can create a mindset that prioritizes short-term gains over long-term strategies and risk management. This can result in impulsive and excessive trading, driven by the need for immediate rewards.

Moreover, the constant pursuit of instant gratification in trading can lead to overconfidence. When we experience a string of successful trades that bring instant rewards, we may start to believe that we have special abilities or superior knowledge, leading us to take greater risks without proper analysis or caution.

Unfortunately, the nature of the financial markets is such that instant success is not guaranteed. The market can be unpredictable, and losses are inevitable. When traders become addicted to the dopamine rush of instant gratification, they may struggle to accept losses and make rational decisions. This can further exacerbate losses and lead to financial and emotional distress.

The quest for instant gratification in trading can negatively impact the brain by reinforcing addictive behaviors, impairing judgment, and increasing the likelihood of excessive risk-taking and losses. It is important for traders to be aware of these potential pitfalls and strive for a balanced and disciplined approach to trading.

The adaptable mindset

A crucial quality for success in trading. Markets are dynamic and ever-changing, and traders must be able to adjust their strategies accordingly. We discuss the necessity of adaptability and how adopting a growth mindset can transform losses into valuable learning opportunities.

Trading can be an emotional rollercoaster, and we address this aspect as well. Fear and greed are two primary emotions that drive market participants, and we delve into their impact on decision-making. We offer strategies for managing these emotions effectively and discuss techniques for emotional self-regulation, such as mindfulness and meditation practices.

Emotional intelligence also plays a significant role in trading. By developing empathy and self-awareness, you can better understand your biases and prejudices that may influence your trading decisions. We explore techniques to enhance self-awareness and foster empathy, enabling you to make more objective assessments of your trading performance.

Finally, we unravel the fascinating world of cognitive biases and their role in trading psychology. These biases, deeply ingrained in our thought processes, can significantly influence our trading behavior and lead to suboptimal outcomes. By recognizing and counteracting these biases, you can make rational decisions and cultivate a disciplined approach to trading, improving your overall performance.

As you immerse yourself in the pages of this book, I encourage you to reflect on your own trading journey. Recognize that success in trading is not merely about technical analysis and market knowledge—it is about understanding yourself, managing your emotions, and developing the mindset of a successful trader.

Prepare to delve into the depths of trading psychology, armed with knowledge and practical strategies to navigate the complex interplay of psychological factors that influence trading decisions. Let this book be your guide as you embark on a journey of self-discovery and self-improvement in pursuit of trading mastery.

Chapter 2: The Emotional Rollercoaster: Understanding Your Trading Mindset

In this chapter, we will embark on a quest to understand the powerful emotions that often accompany trading. By gaining a deep understanding of this emotional rollercoaster, you will learn how to effectively manage your emotions and make rational decisions, even in the face of uncertainty.

As a trader, your mindset plays a crucial role in determining your trading success. The world of trading is brimming with intense emotions that can either propel you towards profitability or lead you astray. So, let's dive deep into understanding your trading mindset and unravel the intricate layers of this emotional rollercoaster.

To begin this voyage of self-discovery, it is crucial to acknowledge and be honest about your current mindset. Remember, knowing and acknowledging are two different things. Many traders fail to recognize the profound impact their emotions have on their decision-making process. By becoming aware of your mindset, you can gain control over your emotions and make rational decisions, even in the face of uncertainty.

Now, let's start with an exercise that will help you gain valuable insights into your trading mindset. Take a moment to jot down the emotions or mindsets you experience while trading. Consider the following examples:

1. Dedication: Do you approach trading with a deep sense of commitment and perseverance? Are you willing to invest the necessary time and effort to achieve your trading goals?

2. Focus: Are you able to fully concentrate on your trading activities? Can you shut out distractions and maintain unwavering focus?

3. Discipline: Are you able to adhere to your trading plan and stick to your predefined rules? Do you possess the self-control necessary to avoid impulsive and reckless trading decisions?

4. Confidence: Do you have faith in your abilities as a trader? Are you confident in your analysis and trading strategies?

5. Detachment to money: Are you able to separate your emotions from the money at stake in your trades? Can you make objective decisions without being influenced by potential gains or losses?

Reflect on each mindset you have identified and contemplate how it affects your trading performance.

Consider the strengths and weaknesses associated with each mindset and how they can impact your decision-making process.

Understanding your trading mindset is the crucial first step towards effectively managing your emotions. By gaining clarity about the emotions that arise during your trading journey, you can develop strategies to harness the positive aspects of each mindset while mitigating the negative ones.

In the chapters to come, we will delve into various emotions and psychological aspects related to trading. We will explore strategies for controlling fear and greed, overcoming cognitive biases, developing self-control, balancing risk perception, making decisions under pressure, building confidence and resilience, managing losses, and much more.

Always remember, trading is not just about numbers and charts; it is also about understanding yourself and how your mind works. Developing a deep understanding of your trading mindset will empower you to navigate the complex world of trading with greater confidence, consistency, and success.

So buckle up and get ready for an insightful journey into the fascinating realm of trading psychology. The emotional rollercoaster awaits, and by the end of this book, you will have the tools and knowledge to ride it

Trading from within: Unleashing your psychological edge

with mastery. Let's begin our expedition towards a more resilient and successful trading mindset.

Chapter 3: Mastering Your Emotions: Controlling Fear and Greed

In the world of trading, two powerful emotions can significantly impact trading outcomes: fear and greed. These emotions often drive traders to make impulsive and irrational decisions, leading to losses and missed opportunities. However, by learning strategies to control fear and greed, traders can cultivate a more disciplined approach to the markets and increase their chances of success. In this chapter, we will delve deep into the psychology of fear and greed, explore their effects on trading decisions, and provide practical techniques to master these emotions.

Section 1: The Impact of Fear on Trading

Fear is a powerful emotion that can greatly affect our trading outcomes. When we perceive threats or dangers in the market, fear kicks in. It can stem from various sources, such as the fear of losing money, missing out on profitable trades, or making wrong decisions. To effectively manage fear, it's important to understand its underlying causes.

Fear can cloud our judgment and lead to irrational decision-making. When fear takes hold, we may find ourselves paralyzed, unable to take the necessary actions. On the other hand, fear can also push us to act impulsively, just to escape the discomfort. It's crucial to recognize how fear biases our thinking and influences our trading decisions.

The fear of loss is one of the most common fears in trading. We become attached to our trades and fear realizing a loss. As a result, we often hold on to losing positions longer than we should, or add to a losing trade. In this section, we will explore techniques to overcome the fear of loss and effectively manage our losses.

To master fear, we need to develop strategies to mitigate its impact on our decision-making. One effective technique is setting predefined stop-loss levels, which help us limit our potential losses. Practicing proper risk management is also crucial. Additionally, maintaining a long-term perspective allows us to see beyond short-term fluctuations and make rational decisions based on sound analysis.

Section 2: The Pitfalls of Greed in Trading

Greed, unlike fear, is driven by an insatiable desire for more. It's that overwhelming urge to maximize profits and take unnecessary risks. In trading, greed can lead us astray, causing us to chase unrealistic gains, ignore warning signs, and deviate from our trading plans.

The consequences of greed can be severe. It blinds us to the risks involved in our trades and makes us susceptible to impulsive decisions. We might enter trades without proper analysis or hold on to winning positions for too long, risking our hard-earned profits.

Recognizing greed within ourselves is a crucial step in overcoming its negative influence. It's important to be aware of signs and behaviors that indicate greed, such as constantly seeking high-risk opportunities, excessive trading, and disregarding risk management rules. By acknowledging its presence, we can take steps to control its impact.

Controlling greed requires discipline and self-awareness. Setting realistic profit targets is one effective strategy. By defining achievable goals, we can resist the temptation to chase unrealistic gains. Adhering to a well-defined trading plan is also crucial. It helps us stay focused and avoid impulsive actions driven by greed. Patience is another key virtue to cultivate, as it prevents us from rushing into trades based on greed-driven impulses. Maintaining a balanced mindset, where we view trading as a long-term journey rather than a quick route to riches, is essential.

Section 3: Achieving Emotional Balance in Trading

Emotional balance is the cornerstone of making rational decisions in trading. It involves recognizing and acknowledging our emotions without allowing them to dictate our actions. Achieving emotional balance requires self-reflection, self-control, and a deep understanding of our own psychological tendencies.

Practicing mindfulness can greatly contribute to emotional balance. By being fully present in the moment and observing our thoughts and feelings without judgment, we can gain clarity and detach ourselves from the influence of fear and greed. In this section, we will delve into mindfulness techniques specifically tailored to trading.

Applying mindfulness techniques to trading can help traders develop a greater sense of presence, focus, and emotional resilience. Here's how you can incorporate the mindful techniques into your trading practice:

1. Mindful Breathing:
- Start each trading session by taking a few moments to focus on your breath. Close your eyes and take deep breaths, paying attention to the sensation of air entering and leaving your body.

- During trading, whenever you feel stressed or overwhelmed, take a pause and bring your attention back to your breath. Allow yourself to fully experience each inhale and exhale, grounding yourself in the present moment.

2. Mindful Observation:

- Practice observing the market without judgment or attachment. Observe the price movements, trends, and patterns with a curious and open mindset.

- Notice any thoughts or emotions that arise while observing the market. Rather than getting carried away by them, simply observe them and let them pass without reacting impulsively.

3. Mindful Awareness:
- Cultivate a heightened sense of awareness during your trading activities. Be fully present and engaged with each trade, monitoring your thoughts, emotions, and physical sensations.

- Notice any biases or preconceived notions that may influence your decision-making. By being aware of these tendencies, you can make more objective and rational trading choices.

4. Mindful Listening:
- Pay attention to the information and news sources you rely on for trading decisions. Practice discernment and critical thinking, rather than blindly following the crowd or reacting to market noise.

- Actively listen to the feedback and insights from other traders, mentors, or experts. Stay open to alternative perspectives and consider them thoughtfully before making trading decisions.

5. Mindful Appreciation:

- Take moments throughout the trading day to express gratitude and appreciate the opportunities that trading presents. This can help foster a positive mindset and reduce the tendency to dwell on losses or setbacks.

- Reflect on the lessons learned from each trade, regardless of the outcome. Focus on personal growth and continuous improvement rather than solely fixating on profits and losses.

Remember, mindfulness is a skill that requires practice and consistency. By incorporating these techniques into your trading routine, you can enhance your ability to stay present, make better decisions, and manage the inevitable ups and downs of the trading journey.

By mastering our emotions and learning to control fear and greed, we can cultivate a more disciplined approach to trading. It's a journey that requires self-awareness, practice, and a commitment to continuous improvement.

Chapter 4: Mastering Awareness and Emotional Balance

In the fast-paced world of trading, it's easy to get caught up in the external factors that influence market movements and trading decisions. However, true mastery of trading comes from within—developing self-awareness and emotional balance that allows you to navigate the markets with clarity and focus. In this chapter, we will explore the importance of unblocking painful information, understanding the role of excitement in trading, embracing mistakes as learning opportunities, avoiding the pitfalls of euphoria and self-sabotage, and finding balance in a world of constant chart-watching.

Section 1: Unblocking Painful Information and Cultivating Awareness

Imagine a scenario where a trader experiences a significant loss on a trade. The pain and disappointment may be overwhelming, leading the trader to block out this painful information and avoid confronting the reasons behind the loss. However, by acknowledging and confronting these painful experiences, we can gain valuable insights and grow as traders.

For example, let's say a trader had a significant loss due to a sudden market reversal. Instead of blocking out the pain and brushing it aside, they take the time to reflect on what went wrong. They analyze their entry and exit points, review their decision-making process, and identify any potential mistakes or miscalculations. By confronting the painful information and learning from it, the trader can make adjustments to their strategy and improve their future trading decisions.

We must remember that one or two losing trades are not the end of the world. We need to constantly remind ourselves that trading is based on probability and requires a large sample size. This means that we should evaluate our success after a couple of months, rather than just a day or two. Short-term results do not provide enough solid data to determine whether we are successful or not.

Section 2: Understanding the Role of Excitement in Trading

Excitement is an inherent part of the trading journey. It's the thrill of the chase, the anticipation of potential gains, and the adrenaline rush that comes with making successful trades. However, unchecked excitement can cloud our judgment and lead to impulsive and reckless decisions.

Consider a scenario where a trader experiences a series of consecutive winning trades. The excitement and euphoria from these wins may tempt them to take on larger positions or deviate from their trading plan. This heightened state of excitement can lead to poor decision-making and unnecessary risks.

To manage excitement, traders can implement strategies such as setting predefined risk percentages and following a well-defined trading plan. For example, a trader may decide to limit their risk to a certain percentage of their overall portfolio, regardless of how successful their recent trades have been. This approach helps them stay grounded and make rational decisions based on risk management principles rather than being driven solely by excitement.

Section 3: Embracing Mistakes as Learning Opportunities

The fear of making mistakes can often lead us to try desperately not to make them. Paradoxically, this fear can actually increase the likelihood of making mistakes. When we are consumed by the fear of failure, we may become overly cautious, indecisive, or prone to analysis paralysis.

Instead of avoiding mistakes, we should embrace them as valuable learning opportunities. For instance, let's say a trader makes a significant error in judgment that results in a loss. Rather than dwelling on the mistake or trying to bury it, they choose to analyze it objectively. They review their decision-making process, identify any biases or emotional influences, and extract lessons from the experience. By embracing mistakes as learning opportunities, traders can grow and improve their trading skills over time.

Section 4: Navigating Euphoria and Avoiding Self-Sabotage

Euphoria, the intense feeling of excitement and success, can be a double-edged sword in trading. While it's natural to feel elated after a series of profitable trades, unchecked euphoria can lead to overconfidence and self-sabotage.

Imagine a trader who experiences a significant winning streak, generating substantial profits. The rush of euphoria may tempt them to deviate from their trading plan and put on large trades without proper analysis. This behavior stems from the addictive allure of excitement and the desire to experience that feeling again. Unfortunately, this pattern often leads to unnecessary risks and eventual losses.

To navigate euphoria, traders must recognize its presence and implement strategies to counteract its influence. For example, they can establish predefined profit targets and discipline themselves to stick to their trading plan. By setting realistic goals and maintaining a balanced mindset, traders can avoid the trap of self-sabotage fueled by euphoria.

Section 5: Finding Balance in the Trading Journey

While dedication and focus are essential in trading, it's important to find balance and avoid becoming consumed by the markets. Sitting behind charts 24/7 may seem like a productive approach, but it often leads to exhaustion, overwhelm, and reduced decision-making abilities.

Consider a trader who spends excessive hours monitoring charts and analyzing market data without taking breaks or engaging in other activities. As time goes on, they experience diminishing returns and increased fatigue, which hampers their overall trading performance.

To find balance, traders should establish a structured trading routine that includes dedicated time for rest, relaxation, and activities unrelated to trading. This can involve setting specific trading hours, engaging in physical exercise, pursuing hobbies, and spending quality time with loved ones. By nurturing a well-rounded life outside of trading, traders can approach the markets with a fresh perspective, renewed energy, and a clearer mindset.

In conclusion, trading from within involves unblocking painful information, understanding the role of excitement, embracing mistakes, avoiding self-sabotage driven by euphoria, and finding balance in the trading journey. By cultivating self-awareness, managing emotions effectively, and maintaining a balanced approach, traders can navigate the markets with greater clarity, focus, and resilience. Remember, true mastery in trading lies not only in external strategies but also in harnessing the power of your inner world.

Chapter 5: Cognitive Biases and Trading: Overcoming Mental Pitfalls

In the world of trading, your decision-making skills can make or break your success. Unfortunately, our judgment is often clouded by cognitive biases, leading us to make poor choices with detrimental outcomes. But fear not! In this chapter, we will dive into various cognitive biases that affect traders and explore strategies to overcome these mental pitfalls. By recognizing and addressing these biases, you, as a trader, can develop a more objective and informed approach to trading.

1. Decision Making Based on Social Media and Trading Platforms:
Let's face it, in today's digital age, social media platforms like Twitter and Telegram, as well as trading platforms like TradingView, have become go-to sources of information for traders. But be cautious! Relying solely on these sources for decision-making can cloud your judgment. The abundance of opinions and ideas can create a herd mentality, where traders blindly follow the crowd without conducting proper analysis. This can be detrimental to your trading account. It's crucial to critically evaluate information from these sources, taking

everything with a grain of salt and not basing your decisions solely on the sentiments expressed by others.

2. The Disposition Effect:
Ah, the disposition effect, a common cognitive bias observed in trading and investing. It's when investors exhibit momentum trading behavior in response to short-term returns and contrarian trading behavior when reacting to long-term returns. This bias is often driven by regret aversion and loss aversion, causing individuals to hold onto losing trades in the hope of a reversal while quickly selling winning trades to secure profits. Overcoming the disposition effect requires discipline and a rational approach to decision-making. Focus on objective criteria and adhere to predetermined exit strategies to avoid being influenced by emotional attachments to trades. Remember, if it's not going your way, take the hint!

3. Mental Shortcuts and Emotional Avoidance:
As human beings, we love shortcuts and want to avoid emotional pain. But in trading, this instinct can lead to mental shortcuts that hinder rational decision-making. You might be tempted to take impulsive actions to avoid losses or secure quick gains instead of following a well-defined trading plan. It's crucial to recognize the impact of emotional biases and consciously work towards making objective decisions based on thorough analysis and adherence to a trading strategy.

4. The Hindsight Bias:

Ah, the hindsight bias, a classic cognitive bias in trading. It's when individuals believe events, even random ones, were more predictable than they actually were. This bias can be particularly dangerous in trading, as it can lead you to believe that you can accurately predict market movements. Falling victim to the hindsight bias can result in overconfidence and excessive risk-taking. To overcome this bias, acknowledge the unpredictable nature of markets and focus on a disciplined approach based on thorough analysis rather than relying on hindsight.

5. Misinformation Effect Bias:

The misinformation effect bias occurs when traders abandon a strategy after experiencing a few consecutive losses, assuming that the strategy is ineffective. This bias disregards the inherent probability and randomness involved in trading outcomes. It's important for you as a trader to distinguish between short-term variations and long-term strategy performance. Instead of hastily abandoning a strategy, assess its effectiveness over an extended period, making data-driven decisions rather than reacting impulsively to temporary setbacks.

6. The Self-Serving Biases:

Traders often succumb to self-serving biases, seeking to attribute their failures to external factors while taking credit for successes. This bias can manifest as blaming the markets for losses, rather than critically evaluating your own trading decisions and strategy. Overcoming self-serving biases requires introspection and a willingness to take responsibility for your actions. Focus on learning from mistakes, maintaining a growth mindset, and continuously improving your skills and strategies.

7. The Availability Heuristic Bias:
The availability heuristic bias stems from placing excessive reliance on easily accessible information, such as historical data when making decisions. While historical data is essential in trading, it's crucial to recognize that past outcomes do not guarantee future results. Traders who fall victim to this bias may prematurely give up on their trading journey, believing that "nothing is working." To overcome this bias, embrace the probabilistic nature of trading and focus on consistently applying sound analysis and risk management techniques.

If there's one thing you should take from this chapter, it's to embrace the probability in the markets.

8. Confirmation Bias
Confirmation bias happens when a trader becomes fixated on either positive or negative market movements, it is often referred to as "confirmation bias" or "candlestick bias." Confirmation bias occurs when individuals seek out or interpret information in a way that supports their existing beliefs or biases, often leading to a narrow focus on specific outcomes.

When a trader experiences confirmation bias while only perceiving green (positive) or red (negative) candles, they tend to ignore or downplay contradictory information or potential opportunities that do not align with their preconceived notions. This tunnel vision can hinder their ability to make rational and objective trading decisions, potentially resulting in missed opportunities or increased risk.

It is important for traders to remain open-minded and consider multiple perspectives when analyzing market data, rather than getting fixated on a singular viewpoint based on the color of the candles.

Overcoming cognitive biases and mental pitfalls is a continuous process that requires self-awareness, discipline, and a commitment to rational decision-making. By recognizing and addressing these biases, you can enhance your judgment and make more objective and informed trading decisions. It's essential to develop a trading plan based on analysis, adhere to predefined strategies, and continuously evaluate and refine your approach to successfully navigate the complexities of the market. By doing so, you can mitigate the negative impact of cognitive biases and increase your chances of achieving long-term trading success.

Chapter 6: Developing a Disciplined Approach: The Importance of Self-Control

The Importance of Self-Control emphasizes the critical role of self-control in trading success. By mastering self-control, traders can resist impulsive actions and adhere to their trading plans, ultimately fostering consistency and discipline.

Self-control is one of the most beneficial characteristics that you can acquire to achieve success. As a trader, mastering self-control allows you to resist impulsive actions and adhere to your trading plans, ultimately fostering consistency and discipline.

In today's world, we are accustomed to instant gratification. We can watch what we want whenever we want, eat anything anytime, and communicate with anyone, regardless of their location. It's easy to believe that we are entitled to immediate satisfaction in all aspects of our lives.

However, when it comes to trading, it's crucial to question your level of discipline and self-control not only in trading but also in your general life.

Can you say no when necessary?

Are you able to control your impulses?

Are you easily swayed?

Do you demonstrate consistency in your goals? Do you follow through with your plans, such as going to the gym as scheduled?

Or does your life revolve around excuses?

Take a moment to assess yourself honestly. Remember, trading is your business if you aspire to be a serious trader—it's not just a hobby.

Do you possess the self-control to stop trading when you need to? Can you trade when it's necessary?

Answering these questions is crucial for your success. If you lack discipline or consistency, it's essential to delve into the reasons behind it. Is it a lack of motivation? Do you easily feel discouraged? If so, it becomes vital to explore what truly motivates you—your goals, dreams, and aspirations. Seek motivation from within, as internal motivation is the only force that will keep burning.

To cultivate self-control, start by practicing it deliberately. Write down a task that you will accomplish tomorrow at a specific time. Choose something that you may not necessarily enjoy doing but that contributes to your overall well-being, such as going to the gym or taking a walk. By breaking the cycle and accomplishing small tasks each day, you can gradually develop discipline and break unproductive habits.

Discipline can be cultivated by incorporating the following strategies:

1. Knowing your strengths and weaknesses: Self-awareness is key to developing discipline. Understand what areas require more focus and take conscious steps to improve them.

2. Removing distractions: Identify and eliminate distractions that hinder your focus and self-control. Minimize the presence of temptations and create an environment conducive to discipline.

3. Setting clear goals and making an execution plan: Define your goals precisely and create a well-structured plan to achieve them. Break down larger goals into smaller, manageable tasks to enhance clarity and progress.

4. Practicing daily diligence and personal accountability: Commit to daily actions that align with your goals. Hold yourself accountable for your actions and ensure you follow through on your commitments.

5. Creating new habits and rituals: Incorporate positive habits and rituals into your daily routine. By consistently

practicing these habits, you reinforce discipline and create a supportive framework for success.

6. Harnessing the power of willpower: Recognize that willpower is a limitless resource that can be replenished each day. Cultivate the habit of positive self-talk to renew and strengthen your willpower daily.

In subsequent chapters, we will delve deeper into the power of words and the impact they have on developing discipline and self-control. The journey to becoming a disciplined trader requires consistent effort, but with determination and the right strategies, you can cultivate the necessary self-control to achieve your goals.

Remember, discipline is a skill that can be developed. Stay committed, persevere through challenges, and celebrate every step forward on your path to trading success.

Chapter 7: The Role of Risk Perception: Balancing Caution and Opportunity

In this chapter, we will dive into the fascinating world of risk perception and its crucial role in trading the markets. As we explore the delicate balance between caution and opportunity, we'll discover how traders can effectively assess risk and make calculated decisions that align with their risk tolerance which you should set before you even start thinking about trading. Think about how much you are willing to lose? Each person has a different psychological risk tolerance. Take a moment now, and assess how much you are willing to risk from your capital and how much you are willing to lose.

One of the most effective ways to understand risk perception is through a risk management simulation. Just like pilots or doctors undergo flight or surgery simulations to enhance their skills and prepare for potential emergencies, traders can benefit from simulating various risk scenarios. These simulations allow traders to experience different market conditions and practice making decisions under pressure, all without risking real capital.

Imagine this: you enter the simulation and find yourself in a highly volatile market where prices are fluctuating wildly. As a trader, you must assess the risks associated with each potential trade. Will you seize the opportunity presented by a sudden price surge, or will you exercise caution and wait for a more stable market? This simulation enables you to experience the emotional and intellectual challenges of navigating risk in real-time, helping you build the skills necessary to balance caution and opportunity effectively.

Another crucial aspect of risk perception is learning from your mistakes. As human beings, we are prone to making errors, and trading is no exception. However, what sets successful traders apart is their ability to analyze and learn from their past mistakes. It's essential to view losses not as failures, but as valuable lessons that provide insight into what went wrong and how to improve and if the trade goes against you despite it being a great set up, remember the market is unpredictable so it is not your fault.

Let's say you made a trade based on a hunch, without conducting thorough analysis. Unfortunately, the trade resulted in a significant loss. Instead of dwelling on the negative outcome, take a step back and ask yourself some key questions: What led you to make that impulsive decision? Did you ignore important risk indicators? Did you sell on a major support level for example? By reflecting on your actions and analyzing the situation, you can uncover valuable insights that will help you refine your trading strategies and mitigate future risks.

Now, let's discuss the concept of exposure when it comes to risk perception. As traders, we must recognize and manage our exposure to different types of risk. This includes market risk, operational risk, and even psychological risk. Each type of risk presents its own challenges, and understanding your susceptibility to these risks is crucial for effective risk management.

For example, market risk refers to the possibility of financial loss due to changes in market conditions. Traders must be aware of market trends, economic indicators, and other external factors that can impact currency prices. Operational risk, on the other hand, involves potential losses arising from internal factors such as system failures, errors in trade execution, or inadequate risk management procedures. By identifying and addressing these risks, traders can implement measures to protect their capital and optimize their trading performance.

Psychological risk, perhaps one of the most underestimated risks, relates to the emotional and mental challenges faced by traders. Fear, greed, and overconfidence and self doubt can cloud judgment and lead to impulsive decisions. By recognizing these psychological factors and developing self-awareness, traders can mitigate the impact of emotions on their decision-making process.

Risk perception plays a pivotal role in forex trading. Through risk management simulations, learning from mistakes, and understanding exposure to different types of risk, traders can strike a balance between caution and opportunity. By cultivating a keen sense of risk perception, you will enhance your ability to assess risks effectively and make calculated trading decisions that align with your risk tolerance. So, let's embrace the challenge of risk perception and embark on the exciting journey of trading with confidence.

Chapter 8: Decision Making Under Pressure

By understanding the impact of pressure on decision-making, traders can develop strategies to stay focused, make rational choices, and avoid costly mistakes.

Have you ever found yourself in a situation where you had to make an important decision under intense pressure? Perhaps it was during a job interview, a crucial exam, or even in a high-stakes game of monopoly. Whatever the context, decision making under pressure can be an incredibly daunting task. In Chapter 8, we will explore the intricacies of decision making under pressure and uncover effective strategies to tackle these challenging situations.

The Impact of Pressure on Decision Making

Pressure, whether internal or external, has a profound effect on our decision-making process. When we feel the weight of expectations, time constraints, or the fear of failure, our cognitive abilities can become compromised. Under pressure, we tend to rely more on intuition and instinct rather than careful analysis. This can lead to impulsive decisions that may not necessarily be in our best interest.

To better understand the impact of pressure on decision making, let's consider an example. Imagine you are a trader in the commodities market, and you are faced with a rapidly changing market situation.

Let's take gold for example, you are interested in purchasing it and it has been experiencing a sudden surge in price, and you must decide whether to buy or wait for a potential dip. The pressure is mounting as you realize that every second counts, and a delay could mean missing out on a lucrative opportunity.

Strategies for Effective Decision Making Under Pressure

1. Stay Calm and Control Your Emotions

One of the key strategies for decision making under pressure is to maintain a calm and composed state of mind. When we allow our emotions to take over, our judgment becomes clouded, and we are more likely to make impulsive decisions. Take a deep breath, step back from the situation, and consciously control your emotions. By remaining calm, you can think more clearly and make rational choices.

For instance, going back to our commodities market example, instead of succumbing to the fear of missing out (FOMO), a trader who can stay calm under pressure is more likely to carefully assess the market trends, evaluate the risks, and make a well-informed decision.

2. Focus on the Process, Not Just the Outcome

When we are under pressure, we often fixate on the desired outcome, which can add to our stress levels and cloud our judgment. To make effective decisions, it is crucial to shift our focus from the outcome to the process itself. By concentrating on the steps and factors that contribute to a good decision, we can enhance our decision-making abilities.

For instance, if you are a student taking a challenging exam, instead of constantly worrying about the final grade, focus on understanding the questions, applying the knowledge you have acquired, and using effective problem-solving techniques. By shifting your attention to the process, you are more likely to perform better and make sound decisions throughout the exam.

3. Gather Information and Seek Different Perspectives

Under pressure, our tendency to rush into decisions without thorough analysis increases. To counteract this inclination, it is essential to gather relevant information and seek different perspectives. This helps to broaden our understanding of the situation, identify potential risks, and consider alternative options.

Let's say you are a manager in a fast-paced work environment, and you need to make a critical decision that will impact your team. Instead of relying solely on your own judgment, seek input from team members, colleagues, or mentors. This collaborative approach can provide valuable insights, challenge your assumptions, and lead to more informed decision making.

4. Practice Decision-Making Under Simulated Pressure

Just as athletes practice under intense conditions to improve their performance, we can also benefit from practicing decision making under simulated pressure. By exposing ourselves to stressful situations in a controlled environment, we can develop the resilience and skills necessary to make better decisions under real pressure.

Chapter 9: Building a Winning Mindset: Confidence and Resilience in Trading

Welcome to Chapter 9: Building a Winning Mindset: Confidence and Resilience in Trading. We're going to dive deep into the world of mindset and explore how confidence and resilience can make all the difference in your trading journey. So, grab a cup of coffee, sit back, and let's get started!

Trading can be a rollercoaster ride, filled with ups and downs. One moment, you're riding high on a winning streak, and the next, you find yourself in the midst of a losing streak that tests your resolve. That's where confidence and resilience come into play. They act as your trusty companions, helping you navigate the challenges and uncertainties that come your way.

Let's start with confidence. Confidence is not just about having an unwavering belief in your abilities; it's about having faith in your trading strategy and trusting your decision-making process. When you have confidence, you can execute your trades without second-guessing yourself. You have the conviction to stick to your plan, even when faced with market volatility or conflicting opinions. In order to achieve confidence in your strategy you can backtest it and even forward testing it, this will give you more confidence in yourself and in your strategy.

Imagine this: You've done your analysis, and your trading strategy signals a promising opportunity. With confidence in your abilities, you take the plunge and enter the trade. As the market fluctuates, you stay calm and collected, knowing that you have thoroughly researched your trade and have faith in your strategy. Even if the trade doesn't go as planned, your confidence keeps you focused, helping you make objective decisions rather than succumbing to emotional reactions.

But confidence alone is not enough. Resilience is the backbone that supports your confidence. It's about being able to bounce back from setbacks, adapt to changing circumstances, and learn from every experience. Resilient traders understand that losses are a part of the game and view them as valuable learning opportunities rather than personal failures.

Let's consider a scenario: You've experienced a string of losses that has left you feeling discouraged and questioning your abilities. A resilient mindset helps you dust yourself off and analyze your trades objectively. You identify areas for improvement, refine your strategy, and get back into the game with renewed determination. Instead of dwelling on past losses, you channel your energy into continuous growth and development.

Confidence and resilience go hand in hand. When you're confident, you're more likely to take calculated risks and stick to your trading plan. And when setbacks occur, resilience helps you bounce back, learn from your mistakes, and adapt your approach.

Building a winning mindset requires consistent effort and practice. Here are a few strategies to help you cultivate confidence and resilience:

1. Knowledge is power: Continuously educate yourself about the markets, build a solid strategy, and master risk management techniques. The more you know, the more confident you'll feel in your decision-making abilities.

2. Embrace a growth mindset: View challenges as opportunities for growth rather than insurmountable obstacles. Every setback is a chance to learn, adapt, and improve.

3. Maintain a trading journal: Keep track of your trades, including the rationale behind each decision and the outcome. This allows you to objectively review your performance, identify patterns, and make necessary adjustments, making adjustments is sometimes necessary because markets are ever changing.

4. Surround yourself with a supportive community: Engage with fellow traders who share your passion for growth and learning. Share experiences, seek advice, and provide support to one another.

5. Practice self-care: Take care of your physical and mental well-being. Exercise regularly, get enough sleep, and manage stress effectively. A healthy mind and body contribute to a resilient mindset.

Remember, developing a winning mindset takes time and patience. There will be ups and downs along the way, but with confidence and resilience, you can weather any storm. Believe in yourself, stay adaptable, and never stop learning. Trust me, your mindset can be the key that unlocks your trading success.

So, my fellow trader, embrace the power of confidence and resilience as you navigate the exciting world of trading. Build a mindset that can withstand any challenge and lead you to long-term success.

Chapter 10: Managing Losses: Strategies for Dealing with Setbacks

Welcome to Chapter 10: Managing Losses: Strategies for Dealing with Setbacks. we're going to dive deep into the psychological aspects of managing losses and explore effective strategies to cope with setbacks.!

First and foremost, it's essential to remember that losses are a normal part of trading. No strategy is 100% accurate, and the market is an unpredictable beast. It's crucial to approach losses with a realistic mindset and understand that they are simply part of the trading journey.

One important aspect to consider is the power of words. The way we talk about losses can significantly impact our emotional state and decision-making process. Instead of saying, "I lost the trade," which implies personal fault or blame, try reframing it as, "The trade didn't go my way." By shifting the language, you detach yourself emotionally from the trade and avoid self-blame. Remember, the market is not a human entity trying to betray you—it's simply a dynamic environment influenced by various factors.

In fact, it's not just the words we use to describe losses that matter; the words we use in general have an impact on our trading and overall mindset. Negative language can breed negativity, affecting how we feel about our strategies and setups. Conversely, positive and empowering language can uplift our mood and strengthen our confidence.

So, be mindful of the words you choose. Use words that reflect a growth mindset and a belief in your ability to learn and adapt. For example, instead of saying, "I'm a terrible trader," reframe it as, "I'm continuously improving my trading skills." These small changes in language can have a profound effect on your overall trading experience..

Remember, managing losses is not about avoiding them altogether; it's about effectively dealing with them when they occur. By reframing your language, practicing risk management, maintaining a trading journal, taking breaks when needed, seeking support, and learning from losses, you can navigate setbacks with resilience and make informed decisions in the face of adversity.

Let's embrace these strategies and develop a mindset that can withstand the challenges of trading. Losses are simply stepping stones on your journey to success. Stay positive, keep learning, and trust in your ability to bounce back.

Chapter 11: Trading and Self-Identity: Exploring the Personal Impact of Success and Failure

In this chapter we will delve into the intricate relationship between trading and self-identity. We will explore how the success or failure experienced in trading can have a profound impact on one's sense of self. By delving into the personal implications of these outcomes, we aim to provide you with insights that can help you maintain a healthy perspective on your trading journey and prevent it from overwhelming your entire being.

Trading, with its ever-changing landscape and unpredictable nature, can be a rollercoaster ride of emotions. When we succeed, it's easy to bask in the glory of our achievements, and we may even begin to define ourselves by our wins. It becomes tempting to believe that our trading prowess defines our self-worth. On the other hand, when we face failure, it can shake the very foundation of our self-identity, leaving us questioning our abilities and feeling a profound sense of disappointment.

To fully grasp the impact of success and failure on our self-identity, let's consider a few live examples that highlight different aspects of this complex relationship.

Example 1: The Rise and Fall of a Trader's Ego
Imagine a trader who experiences a series of successful trades, consistently making profitable decisions. Their self-identity becomes closely intertwined with their trading prowess. They begin to see themselves as a "master" trader, someone who is invincible and always on top. However, this inflated self-perception can blind them to potential risks and lead to reckless decision-making. When the market eventually turns against them, they suffer significant losses, shaking the very core of their self-identity. They may experience feelings of shame, worthlessness, and a loss of purpose, as they grapple with the fact that their success was not as enduring as they once believed.

Example 2: Resilience and Adaptability
Contrastingly, let's consider a trader who faces a string of failures. Instead of letting these setbacks define their self-worth, they view them as valuable learning opportunities. They understand that failure is an inherent part of the trading journey and does not define their abilities as a trader or their worth as a person. This trader maintains a healthy perspective by recognizing that success and failure are not absolutes but rather fluctuating states in the ever-evolving market. They adapt their strategies, continuously learn, and remain resilient in the face of adversity. Their self-identity

remains intact, rooted in a deep understanding that their value extends beyond the outcomes of their trades.

Example 3: Finding Balance and Purpose
Lastly, let's explore a trader who strikes a delicate balance between their trading activities and their broader sense of self. They acknowledge the importance of their trading successes and failures but do not allow these outcomes to consume their entire identity. Instead, they cultivate a diverse range of interests and relationships that bring them fulfillment and joy outside the world of trading. By doing so, they are able to maintain perspective, appreciate the lessons learned from trading, and recognize their inherent worth as a multi-faceted individual.

As you navigate the tumultuous world of trading, it is crucial to remember that your self-identity is not solely defined by your successes or failures in this realm. Trading is merely one aspect of your life, albeit an important one. By maintaining a healthy perspective, embracing resilience, and cultivating a well-rounded sense of self, you can weather the storms of the market and remain grounded in your intrinsic worth.

In the next chapter, we will delve into the social aspects of trading. Until then, remember that you are more than your trading results, and your self-identity is a tapestry woven from a myriad of experiences.

Chapter 12: The Social Aspect of Trading: Emotional Contagion and Herding Behavior

In this chapter, we will explore the powerful influence of social interactions on trading decisions. Understanding the concepts of emotional contagion and herding behavior can help you navigate the social dynamics of the market and avoid falling victim to herd mentality. As a trader, it is crucial to trade from within and make independent, well-informed decisions based on your own analysis and strategy.

Herding behavior is a phenomenon observed in financial markets where individuals tend to follow the actions and decisions of a larger group, often without considering their own independent judgment. This behavior can be fueled by a fear of missing out or a desire for safety in numbers. As tempting as it may be to join the herd, it is essential to recognize the potential risks and pitfalls associated with this mindset.

One of the key sources of herding behavior in today's digital age is the abundance of trading signals and recommendations shared within various groups and communities. Social media platforms such as Twitter,

Instagram, and YouTube have become popular avenues for traders to exchange ideas, share tips, and discuss market trends. While these platforms can provide valuable insights, it is crucial to exercise caution and not blindly follow the crowd.

When it comes to trading signals shared within groups, it is important to conduct your due diligence and validate the information independently. Remember that not all signals or recommendations are created equal, and blindly relying on them can lead to disastrous outcomes. Instead, take the time to understand the rationale behind a trade recommendation and assess whether it aligns with your own trading strategy and risk tolerance.

Social media platforms, in particular, can be breeding grounds for emotional contagion. Emotional contagion refers to the phenomenon where individuals' emotions and behaviors are influenced by those around them. In the context of trading, this means that the emotions expressed by others on social media can affect your own trading decisions. If you see a flood of posts expressing extreme optimism or pessimism about a particular asset, it is natural to feel compelled to act accordingly.

Massive gains showcased on social media can have negative consequences for traders. It is important to recognize that these extraordinary profits are often unrealistic or necessitate substantial capital. When encountering a video claiming, "I made $50,000 from

$100," exercise caution because while it may be achievable, it is unlikely to be replicable. Realistic risk assessment aligns with the actuality of trading. Many individuals exhibit only the positive aspects of their trading to attract a larger following, promote their courses, or signal groups. Only a few people disclose their entire portfolio, offering a complete and accurate picture of their trading performance. It is crucial to approach such social media posts with skepticism and maintain a grounded perspective on the challenges and complexities of trading.

However, it is crucial to remain grounded and not let the emotions of others dictate your trading strategy. Emotions such as fear and greed can cloud judgment and lead to impulsive decisions. Remember that successful trading requires a disciplined and rational approach. Instead of being swayed by the emotions of others, focus on your own analysis, risk management, and adherence to your trading plan.

To trade from within, you must develop the ability to filter out noise and distractions caused by herding behavior and emotional contagion. This involves cultivating a strong sense of self-awareness and maintaining an independent mindset. By doing so, you can stay true to your own trading principles and avoid being swept away by the irrational exuberance or panic of the crowd.

In conclusion, the social aspect of trading cannot be ignored. Emotional contagion and herding behavior have a significant impact on market dynamics, we can see this most evidently in Cryptocurrencies where it all depends on what people think and the hype around it. By understanding these phenomena and consciously guarding against them, you can make more informed and independent trading decisions. Remember to always trade from within, relying on your own analysis and strategy rather than blindly following the crowd. Stay disciplined, remain rational, and let your own trading journey be guided by your unique perspective and insights.

Chapter 13: Trading and Cognitive Performance: Enhancing Mental Sharpness

Welcome to Chapter 13 of "Trading from Within" In this chapter, we will delve into the crucial connection between cognitive performance and trading success. By understanding and implementing strategies to enhance your mental sharpness, you can significantly improve your decision-making abilities, focus, and overall performance as a trader.

To start with, let's address the importance of sleep. Many traders underestimate the impact of quality sleep on their cognitive functioning. Sleep deprivation can lead to reduced alertness, impaired concentration, and increased risk-taking behavior. It is vital to prioritize getting adequate sleep to ensure your brain is well-rested and ready for the challenges of the trading day.

Consider incorporating a consistent sleep routine into your daily life. Aim for a sufficient number of hours of sleep and create a relaxing bedtime ritual. Avoid electronic devices and stimulating activities before bed, as they can disrupt your sleep patterns. By prioritizing restful sleep, you will enhance your cognitive abilities and make better trading decisions.

Next, let's discuss the role of nutrition in optimizing cognitive performance. The food you consume has a direct impact on your brain function. Incorporating a balanced and nutritious diet can boost your mental clarity, focus, and energy levels. Make sure to include foods rich in omega-3 fatty acids, antioxidants, and vitamins to support brain health.

Consider incorporating brain-boosting foods such as fatty fish, avocados, blueberries, and dark chocolate into your diet. These foods are known to enhance memory, concentration, and overall cognitive function. Additionally, stay hydrated by drinking plenty of water throughout the day, as dehydration can impair cognitive performance.

Physical exercise is another powerful tool for enhancing cognitive performance. Regular exercise not only improves physical fitness but also benefits your brain. Engaging in cardiovascular activities like running, swimming, or cycling increases blood flow to the brain, promoting the growth of new neurons and enhancing cognitive abilities.

Make exercise a part of your daily routine. Whether it's a brisk walk, yoga session, or hitting the gym, find an activity that you enjoy and commit to it. Not only will you boost your mental sharpness, but you'll also reduce stress and improve overall well-being, enabling you to approach trading with a clear and focused mind.

Apart from these physical aspects, it's essential to address the spiritual dimension of your life. Cultivating spirituality can provide a sense of inner peace, clarity, and emotional well-being, which directly influence cognitive performance. Practices like meditation, mindfulness, or engaging in activities that align with your beliefs can enhance mental clarity and focus.

Take time each day to engage in spiritual practices that resonate with you. This could involve meditation, prayer, journaling, or spending time in nature. By nurturing your spiritual side, you create a foundation of mental calmness and clarity that will positively impact your trading decisions.

In conclusion, enhancing your mental sharpness is a multifaceted approach that involves taking care of various aspects of your life. Prioritizing sleep, consuming a balanced diet, engaging in regular exercise, and nurturing your spiritual well-being are all essential components of optimizing your cognitive performance as a trader.

By implementing these strategies, you will sharpen your decision-making abilities, improve focus, and achieve greater trading success. Remember, trading is not just about analyzing charts and numbers; it's also about cultivating a healthy and vibrant mind that can navigate the complexities of the financial markets.

Trading from within: Unleashing your psychological edge

Take the time to invest in your mental sharpness, and you will reap the rewards in your trading journey.

Chapter 14: Overcoming Analysis Paralysis: Finding Clarity in Information Overload

In the world of trading, information is abundant. Market news, economic data, technical indicators, and expert opinions flood our screens and fill our minds. As traders, we are constantly bombarded with a deluge of information, which can lead to a state of analysis paralysis. This overwhelming influx of data often leaves us feeling stuck, indecisive, and unable to make clear and timely trading decisions.

Chapter 14: Overcoming Analysis Paralysis: Finding Clarity in Information Overload is dedicated to helping you navigate through this sea of information and regain your clarity in trading. It is essential to understand that the goal is not to accumulate every piece of information available or to perfect a trading strategy to an unattainable level. Instead, we must focus on developing the ability to filter out the noise and identify the most relevant information for our trading decisions.

One of the first steps in overcoming analysis paralysis is to acknowledge that no strategy can guarantee a 100% win rate. Trading involves uncertainty, and even the most well-researched and proven strategies can experience losses. It is crucial to accept this reality and approach trading with a mindset of managing risks rather than seeking perfection.

Imagine a scenario where you have a trading strategy that has proven successful over time. However, you come across new indicators or techniques that seem promising and are tempted to add them to your strategy. While it's important to stay informed and open to new ideas, adding too many indicators can lead to information overload and confusion. It's like drowning in a sea of charts and signals, unable to see the shore.

To overcome analysis paralysis, you must strike a balance between acquiring knowledge and applying it effectively. Instead of constantly searching for the "holy grail" of trading, focus on understanding the core principles and concepts that drive the markets. Develop a deep understanding of a few key indicators that resonate with your trading style and goals. Remember, it's not about the quantity of information you possess, but the quality and relevance of the information you utilize.

Let's consider an example to illustrate this point. Suppose you are an Intra-day trader who primarily relies on trend-following indicators such as moving averages and trend lines. You come across a new indicator called the "XYZ oscillator" that claims to provide superior entry and exit signals. The temptation to add this indicator to your strategy may be strong, but it's crucial to assess whether it aligns with your existing approach and if it truly adds value.

Take the time to thoroughly study the new indicator, its underlying principles, and its historical performance. Compare it to your current indicators and evaluate whether it provides unique and complementary insights. If it passes these tests, you can consider integrating it into your strategy. However, if it complicates your decision-making process or dilutes the effectiveness of your existing indicators, it's best to resist the urge and maintain focus on what has already proven successful for you.

Remember, clarity in trading comes from simplicity and a deep understanding of the core principles. By reducing the noise and filtering out irrelevant information, you can develop a clear and concise evaluation process. Embrace the fact that you cannot know everything or predict every market movement with certainty. Instead, focus on making informed decisions based on a few key indicators and sound risk management principles.

In conclusion, Chapter 14: Overcoming Analysis Paralysis: Finding Clarity in Information Overload empowers you to navigate through the overwhelming sea of information in trading. By resisting the urge to chase after every new indicator or piece of advice, you can filter out the noise and identify the most relevant information for your trading decisions. Remember, it's not about perfection or accumulating endless knowledge, but about finding clarity in simplicity and making informed choices based on a solid foundation of understanding.

Chapter 15: The Role of Intuition in Trading: Trusting Your Gut Instincts

To effectively integrate it into your trading strategy. In this chapter, we will explore the power of intuition, provide practical tips for developing and honing your intuitive abilities, and demonstrate how trusting your gut instincts can lead to profitable trading opportunities.

Intuition, often referred to as a "gut feeling" or "sixth sense," is an innate ability that resides within each of us. It's that subtle inner voice that guides us when we navigate uncertain terrain. While trading is often associated with numbers, charts, and analysis, intuition plays a significant role in decision-making.

Think about a time when you made a trade solely based on a gut feeling. Perhaps you had a hunch about a particular forex pair, even though the data suggested otherwise. Against all odds, your intuition was spot on, and you reaped the rewards. These moments are not mere coincidences but rather a testament to the power of intuition in trading.

Intuition operates on a level that transcends conscious reasoning. It taps into your subconscious mind, which processes vast amounts of information and experiences. It's a culmination of your past experiences, knowledge, and emotions, distilled into an intuitive signal that guides your decision-making process.

Trusting your gut instincts in trading requires practice and fine-tuning. Here are a few techniques to help you develop your intuitive abilities:

1. Mindfulness and Self-Awareness: Take time to cultivate mindfulness and self-awareness. By quieting your mind and paying attention to your thoughts and emotions, you can become more attuned to your intuitive signals. Meditation, journaling, and reflection exercises can aid in this process.

2. Validate Your Intuition: Keep a trading journal where you record your intuitive signals and the outcomes of your trades. Over time, you'll be able to discern patterns and validate the accuracy of your gut feelings. This will help build confidence in your intuitive abilities.

3. Trust Your Body's Reactions: Pay attention to how your body responds to certain trading decisions. Do you feel a knot in your stomach or a sense of excitement? These physical sensations can be valuable cues from your intuition. Learn to trust your body's reactions and use them as a guide in your trading journey.

4. Practice Patience and Discernment: Intuition often speaks softly amidst the noise of the market. Learn to distinguish between genuine intuitive signals and impulsive emotions. Exercise patience and discernment

when making trading decisions based on your gut instincts.

Let's consider an example to illustrate the role of intuition in trading. Imagine you're analyzing a GBPUSD that appears to be a strong buy according to your technical analysis. However, something doesn't feel right, maybe it is starting to form a range. Your intuition sends a subtle signal, warning you to hold off on the trade. Despite the compelling numbers, you decide to trust your gut and refrain from entering the market.

A few hours later, news breaks out about a change in interest rates. GBPUSD plummets, and those who followed the technical analysis blindly suffer heavy losses. By trusting your intuition, you avoided a potential disaster and preserved your capital.

Remember, intuition is a skill that can be honed and refined with practice. The more you trust and rely on your gut instincts, the more finely attuned you become to the subtle signals guiding your trading decisions. It's not about disregarding analytical tools but rather embracing a holistic approach that combines both rational analysis and intuitive insights.

By developing your intuitive abilities and learning to trust your gut instincts, you can enhance your decision-making process and uncover profitable trading opportunities. So, listen to that inner voice, cultivate your intuition, and trade from within.

Chapter 16: Time Perspective and Trading: Balancing Short-Term and Long-Term Thinking

In this chapter, we will delve into a crucial aspect of trading: time perspective. The ability to balance short-term and long-term thinking is vital for success in the dynamic world of trading, whether you are involved in forex, indices or stocks. By finding the right equilibrium between these two perspectives, you can enhance your decision-making process and increase your overall trading performance.

When it comes to trading, it's easy to get caught up in the excitement of short-term gains or losses. The rapid fluctuations in prices and the constant flow of market news can create a sense of urgency that pushes us to make impulsive decisions. However, focusing solely on short-term outcomes can often lead to hasty trades that are not aligned with our overall trading strategy.

On the other hand, disregarding short-term opportunities in favor of long-term goals can cause us to miss out on profitable trades. Long-term thinking allows us to identify and capitalize on trends that can yield substantial profits over time. By considering the bigger picture, we can make informed decisions that align with our trading objectives. This applies even if you are trading on a shorter time frame.

Let's consider a forex trading example to illustrate the importance of balancing short-term and long-term thinking. Imagine you have been closely monitoring the EUR/USD currency pair, and based on your analysis, you believe the euro is likely to strengthen against the US dollar in the long run. However, in the short term, there is a significant event scheduled that could potentially weaken the euro. Without a balanced time perspective, you might be tempted to disregard the short-term risk and enter a trade based solely on your long-term outlook. This approach could expose you to unnecessary losses if the short-term event does impact the euro negatively. On the other hand, if you focus solely on short-term fluctuations, you might miss out on the potential gains that the long-term trend offers.

To find the optimal balance, it's crucial to assess each trade based on its own merits and take into account both short-term and long-term factors depending on the time frame you are trading. One approach is to use technical analysis to identify short-term entry and exit points while keeping your long-term goals in mind. By doing so, you can take advantage of short-term opportunities that align with your overall trading strategy.

Another effective strategy is to diversify your trading portfolio by incorporating both short-term and long-term positions. By allocating a portion of your capital to short-term trades, you can actively respond to market fluctuations and take advantage of potential quick profits. Simultaneously, maintaining long-term positions allows you to capitalize on broader market trends and potentially achieve substantial gains over time.

Ultimately, finding the right balance between short-term and long-term thinking requires discipline, patience, and a clear understanding of your trading goals. Remember to regularly assess your trades, re-evaluate your time perspective, and make adjustments as needed. Flexibility and adaptability are essential traits for successful traders.

In conclusion, Chapter 16 has highlighted the significance of balancing short-term and long-term thinking in trading. By adopting a balanced time perspective, you can make informed decisions that align with your goals and adapt to different market conditions. Remember, trading is a marathon, not a sprint, and finding the right balance between short-term gains and long-term profitability is the key to sustainable success.

Chapter 17: Trading Psychology and System Development: Aligning Strategies with Personal Traits

In this chapter, we will delve into the crucial aspect of aligning your trading strategies with your personal traits. Recognizing your strengths, weaknesses, and individual psychology is instrumental in developing trading systems that are perfectly suited to your unique characteristics. By doing so, you can significantly enhance your chances of success in the world of trading, be it in forex, indices, or any other financial market.

When it comes to trading, there is no one-size-fits-all approach. Different trading styles exist, and it is essential to choose the one that resonates with your personality and aligns with your goals. Let's explore a few popular trading styles to help you identify what might be right for you.

1. Scalping:
Scalping is a trading style that focuses on short-term trades, aiming to capitalize on small price movements. Scalpers typically enter and exit trades within minutes or even seconds, aiming to make small profits on

numerous trades throughout the day. This style requires a high level of concentration, discipline, and the ability to make quick decisions. If you are someone who thrives in fast-paced environments and can handle the pressure of rapid decision-making, scalping might be the right fit for you.

For example, imagine you are trading forex and notice a currency pair. As a scalper, you would enter the trade, take advantage of the small price fluctuations, and exit with a small profit within a couple of minutes.

2. Intra-day Trading:
Intra-day trading involves holding positions for a few hours to a full trading day, aiming to capture larger price movements within that time frame. Traders who prefer this style often analyze charts, technical indicators, and market trends to identify potential opportunities. Intra-day traders need to be disciplined, patient, and capable of managing their emotions, as positions can fluctuate during the trading day. If you enjoy analyzing charts and have the ability to stay focused throughout the day, intra-day trading might suit you well.

For instance, let's say you are trading indices and notice a strong bullish trend forming on a specific index. As an intra-day trader, you would enter a long position, anticipating further upside movement, and exit the trade before the end of the trading day to secure your profits.

3. Swing Trading:

Swing trading involves holding positions for several days to weeks, aiming to capture medium-term price movements. Swing traders often rely on technical analysis, fundamental factors, and market sentiment to identify potential trades. This style requires patience, the ability to withstand short-term market fluctuations, and the discipline to stick to your trading plan. If you prefer a more relaxed trading approach and have the patience to wait for profitable setups, swing trading might be the ideal fit for you.

For example, suppose you are trading forex and notice a currency pair approaching a strong support level. As a swing trader, you would wait for confirmation of a reversal, enter a long position, and hold it until the price reaches a predetermined target or shows signs of reversing again.

Remember, these examples are just a starting point to help you understand different trading styles. It is crucial to explore each style further, assess your strengths and weaknesses, and experiment with paper trading or small real trades to find the style that suits you best.

By aligning your trading strategies with your personal traits, you can establish a solid foundation for success in the markets. Take the time to understand yourself, your risk tolerance, and your preferred timeframes. Combine this self-awareness with a thorough understanding of the chosen trading style, and you will be on your way to trading from within.

You need to understand that trading is a dynamic endeavor that requires careful consideration of individual strengths and weaknesses. As a trader, I have noticed for example that I tend to be a better seller than a buyer. After analyzing my selling trades, I have consistently achieved better results compared to my long trades. I have developed an ability to identify weaknesses in the markets more effectively than strengths. Psychologically, my brain naturally approaches things from a selling perspective due to my personal background in sales, which is an important factor to understand. Understanding one's strengths and weaknesses in trading is essential for optimizing decision-making and ultimately achieving success in the ever-evolving world of financial markets.

Chapter 18: Risk Management: Safeguarding Your Trading Journey

In the world of trading, risk management plays a pivotal role in determining the success or failure of your trading journey. It acts as a shield, protecting you from potentially devastating losses and ensuring that your trading decisions are rational, well-calculated, and aligned with your overall financial goals. Within this chapter, we will explore the significance of risk management and how it can help you navigate the tumultuous waters of the trading market.

Imagine you have a trading account with $10,000. The first step in effective risk management is to identify the amount of money you can afford to lose without triggering negative psychological reactions or succumbing to detrimental habits, such as seeking revenge. It is crucial to establish a predetermined risk percentage that aligns with your risk tolerance level. This percentage represents the maximum amount you are willing to risk on any single trade.

For example, let's say you decide on a risk percentage of 2%. This means that on each trade, you are prepared to lose a maximum of $200 (2% of $10,000). By adhering to this predetermined risk percentage, you create a psychological buffer that prevents emotional decision-making based on losses. This buffer helps you maintain a disciplined approach, regardless of market conditions or individual trade outcomes.

While engaging in news trading can offer enticing opportunities, it also carries inherent risks due to slippage and market gaps. Slippage occurs when the execution price of a trade differs from the expected price, often resulting in unexpected losses. Therefore, it is essential to exercise caution when trading during periods of significant news announcements or market volatility. Consider implementing stricter risk management measures during such times to mitigate potential losses.

It's important to note that different individuals possess varying levels of risk tolerance. Some people are more comfortable taking risks and are more inclined to tolerate potential losses, while others are inherently risk-averse and prefer to prioritize capital preservation. Your risk tolerance is influenced by your personality traits, experiences, and financial goals. It's crucial to understand your own risk tolerance and design a risk management strategy that aligns with your comfort level.

Another aspect of risk management is maintaining a favorable risk-to-reward ratio. This ratio refers to the potential profit you expect to gain from a trade compared to the amount you are willing to risk. It is generally recommended to aim for a minimum ratio of

1:1 or higher, especially if you have a consistently high win rate. For instance, if you possess an approximate 80% winning rate, a risk-to-reward ratio of 1:1 means that you aim to earn at least the same amount as your risk on each trade. However, having a lower winning rate would mean that you have to increase your reward and the ratio then will be 1:1.5 or higher.

By maintaining a positive risk-to-reward ratio, you ensure that your potential profits outweigh your potential losses over the long run. This strategic approach helps you achieve profitability even if a portion of your trades results in losses. It also enables you to recover and thrive in the face of temporary setbacks.

In summary, risk management is an integral part of your trading journey, providing protection against devastating losses and helping you maintain discipline and objectivity in decision-making. By identifying your risk tolerance, setting predetermined risk percentages, being cautious during news trading, and maintaining a favorable risk-to-reward ratio, you can navigate the trading market with confidence and increase your chances of long-term success. Remember, the key to achieving sustainable profits lies not only in your trading skills but also in your ability to effectively manage risk.

Chapter 19: From Novice to Expert: The Psychology of Skill Acquisition in Trading

In this chapter, we will delve into the intriguing world of skill acquisition in trading and explore the pivotal role that psychology plays in this process. As you embark on this journey, keep in mind that trading is not just about numbers and charts; it is equally about understanding your own mind and emotions.

Becoming a proficient trader requires more than just technical knowledge and market analysis. It demands a deep understanding of oneself and the ability to navigate the psychological challenges that arise throughout the journey. By recognizing and embracing the stages of skill development, you can accelerate your progress and transform from a novice to an expert.

The first stage of skill acquisition is the Novice stage. At this point, you are just beginning your trading journey, full of excitement and curiosity. However, you may also feel overwhelmed by the vast amount of information and the complexity of the markets. It is crucial to remember that every successful trader started as a novice. Embrace this stage and focus on building a strong foundation of knowledge and skills. Take advantage of educational resources, attend trading seminars, and immerse yourself in the trading community. By doing so, you will gradually develop a solid understanding of market dynamics and trading strategies.

As you progress, you will enter the Intermediate stage. This is where you start gaining practical experience and putting your knowledge into action. You may face a series of ups and downs, as losses and wins become part of your trading journey. It is important to cultivate resilience and discipline during this stage. Keep a trading journal to reflect on your trades, identify patterns, and learn from both your successes and failures. This introspective approach will enable you to fine-tune your strategies and develop a robust trading plan.

The Advanced stage marks a significant milestone in your trading journey. At this point, you have accumulated substantial experience and expertise. Your decision-making process becomes more intuitive, and you start developing a personal trading style. However, complacency can be a silent threat. It is essential to continuously seek growth and improvement. Expand your knowledge by exploring different trading instruments such as Forex or indices. Experiment with new strategies and risk management techniques. Remember, the markets are constantly evolving, and so should your trading approach.

Finally, we arrive at the Expert stage. This is the pinnacle of skill acquisition, where you have honed your abilities and developed a deep understanding of the markets. As an expert trader, you possess a remarkable level of confidence, discipline, and emotional intelligence. However, even at this stage, there is always room for growth and adaptation. Stay humble and remain open to new ideas and perspectives. Engage with other traders, attend online seminars, and participate in forums to continue expanding your knowledge and refining your skills.

To illustrate these concepts, let's take a look at a couple of examples from the Forex and indices markets:

Forex Example: Imagine you are an intermediate trader who has been consistently studying and practicing various Forex strategies. You have identified a trend in a currency pair and decide to enter a trade based on your analysis. However, the market suddenly experiences a sharp reversal, resulting in a significant loss. Instead of becoming disheartened, you take a step back and analyze the trade objectively. By maintaining a growth mindset, you identify potential flaws in your strategy and adjust your risk management approach. This experience strengthens your resilience and teaches you valuable lessons about adapting to market conditions.

Commodities Example: As an expert trader specializing in commodities, you have developed a unique trading style based on technical indicators and market sentiment. You notice an impending economic event that could significantly impact the global markets. Through careful analysis and anticipation, you make strategic adjustments to your positions, minimizing potential risks and capitalizing on opportunities. Your expertise allows you to navigate volatile market conditions and make informed decisions, even in the face of uncertainty.

Remember, dear reader, skill acquisition in trading is a journey that requires self-reflection, continuous learning, and adaptability. Embrace each stage and embrace the challenges that come your way. By mastering the psychology of skill acquisition, you can progress from a novice trader to an expert, transforming yourself into a successful and resilient trader.

Chapter 20: Beyond Profit and Loss: Finding Meaning and Fulfillment in Trading

As we come to the end of this book, I want to express my deepest gratitude for accompanying us on this journey of exploring the world of trading. We have delved into various aspects of this complex and ever-evolving field, and I hope that you have gained valuable insights and knowledge along the way.

In this final chapter, we have ventured beyond the realm of profit and loss, recognizing that trading is about much more than just monetary gains. It is about finding meaning and fulfillment in our actions, aligning our trading goals with our values, and making a positive impact on our own lives and the lives of others.

I urge you to remember that your trading journey begins within yourself. Take the time to know yourself, understand your motivations, and identify what truly drives you. By doing so, you can establish a strong foundation for your trading endeavors.

In addition to self-awareness, risk management, discipline, and consistency are essential components of successful trading. Stay committed to your chosen strategy, both in your trading activities and in your life as a whole. Consistency breeds success, and the discipline to adhere to your plan is paramount.

Never forget that setbacks and challenges are part of the trading journey. Most people fail not because of their strategy or analytical skills, but because they lack the psychological capabilities to maintain consistency, discipline, and resilience. Learn from your losses, embrace the unpredictability of the markets, and accept that losses are inevitable. It is through these experiences that you will grow and evolve as a trader.

Luck plays no significant role in trading. It is your analysis, your understanding of probabilities, and your ability to manage risks that truly matter. Do not dwell on missed opportunities or losing trades; instead, focus on learning and adapting and make your loss fuel your hunger for success. Develop the psychological strength to handle the ups and downs of the market, and maintain a mindset that is not burdened by emotional reactions.

Remember, trading is not solely about profit and loss. It is about unleashing your potential, searching within yourself, and finding the discipline and consistency required for success. These qualities are not only valuable in trading but also in all areas of your life. Embrace the challenges, regulate your emotions, and push yourself forward with determination and resilience.

Fulfillment in trading comes from being at peace with your journey, riding its waves without being overwhelmed by negative emotions and disappointments. Engage in this exhilarating environment with detachment, as excessive excitement or emotional attachment can cloud your judgment. Seek a state of calm and boredom, for it is within that state that you are truly in control of your actions and decisions.

As we part ways, I wish you purpose, fulfillment, and meaningful trades ahead. May you continue to explore the depths of trading, always remembering that success lies not only in financial gains but also in personal growth, self-discovery, and the impact you make on the world around you.

May your trading endeavors be filled with wisdom, resilience, and abundance.

About the Author

Hello there! We are Fouad and Joud, a dynamic husband and wife duo with a shared passion for the financial markets. Allow us to introduce ourselves and give you a glimpse of our background.

Fouad:

I am a Mechanical Engineering graduate with a diverse professional background. After working in engineering for five years, I found myself drawn to the world of cryptocurrencies and financial markets. I took a leap of faith and began trading in the Forex markets, which eventually led me to explore various trading strategies and techniques. With six years of experience under my belt, I've honed my skills and gained valuable insights into the intricacies of trading. I have worked with various brokers in the UK and helped many people with their trading journey by listening to the struggles of traders. I understood that the key lies in psychology and the mindset.

Joud:

My journey has been focused on business and strategic planning. I hold an MBA degree in Strategic Planning and have dedicated a decade of my professional life to the field of Marketing. Alongside my marketing expertise, I developed a deep interest in psychology and its influence on human behavior. I pursued my passion by obtaining a diploma in psychology and completing a certificate program at Harvard University, specializing in Emotions.

Before diving into the world of trading, I had the opportunity to observe and learn from my husband, Fouad, as he navigated the financial markets. This experience provided me with a unique understanding of the psychological aspects that play a significant role in trading.

Together:

Motivated by our combined knowledge and experiences, we decided to embark on a journey to help aspiring traders unlock their full potential. Our aim is to blend our respective areas of expertise and passion to create a comprehensive guide that addresses the challenges traders face in the financial markets.

In our guide, you can expect a harmonious fusion of deep understanding of the psychological factors that influence decision-making and risk management along with techniques to overcome psychological obstacles of trading. We firmly believe that by equipping traders with a holistic understanding of the financial markets and providing them with the necessary tools to control their mindset and trade from within, we can empower them to make informed decisions and achieve their trading goals.

We are excited to share our expertise and insights with you, providing a roadmap to navigate the complex world of trading. Thank you for joining us on this transformative journey, and we hope our guide helps you reach new heights in your trading endeavors.

Yours Truly,

Fouad and Joud

www.ingramcontent.com/pod-product-compliance
Lightning Source LLC
Chambersburg PA
CBHW020455220526
45464CB00002B/1001